THE GESTALT APPROACH

AN INTRODUCTION FOR MANAGERS AND TRAINERS

2ND EDITION

NEIL CLARK and TONY FRASER

ROFFEY PARK
MANAGEMENT COLLEGE

Published by:

> Roffey Park Management College
> Forest Road
> Horsham
> West Sussex, RH12 4TD
> United Kingdom

Distributed Exclusively in North America by:

> *The Gestalt Journal*
> P. O. Box 990
> Highland, New York 12528-0990
> (914) 691-7192

ISBN 0-939266-12-1

Price $8.00 US

For Information On Quantity Discounts, Contact:

> *The Gestalt Journal*

CONTENTS

PREFACE TO THE SECOND EDITION

When this booklet was published in 1982 the two major aims of the authors were, one, to communicate to a wider audience our experiences in, and enthusiasm for, the Gestalt Approach; and, two, to provide a brief introduction to interested people who had no knowledge or particular interest in the broader areas of humanistic psychology or therapy.

Five years later these still remain the major aims of this edition. In addition to a number of changes in the text to incorporate new material and experiences an extra chapter 'Developments in Gestalt' has also been included. This chapter describes how Gestalt has developed since the early 1960's at Esalen and how it is currently being used in both the fields of therapy and training.

This booklet is written for those who have little or no knowledge in this area and describes the origins of Gestalt (Chap. 1); some of the basic theory (Chaps. 2-4); our use of Gestalt in the context of management training (Chaps. 5-6); recent developments in Gestalt (Chap. 7); and offers some exercises for individuals who want to increase their level of self-awareness (Chap. 8).

I would like to take the opportunity to thank those who have helped in the preparation of this edition. First, I would like to thank Roffey Park Management College, particularly John Giles and Robin Evenden for their continuing support and encouragement. I would also like to thank the secretaries at the College for their patience and hard work in typing the revised material. Finally, I would like to thank the training staff of the Gestalt Therapy Institute of Los Angeles for their important contribution to my understanding and practice of Gestalt.

Neil Clark

February 1987

Note. This booklet has necessarily been written from male experience and this is reflected in a number of ways — not least in the use of the convention of male pronouns. Use of this convention is not intended to exclude women.

CHAPTER 1

INTRODUCTION

The word 'gestalt' is German and is difficult to translate precisely into English. Roughly it means 'form', 'pattern' or 'configuration', and refers to the process of integrating a series of detailed perceptions into a complete experience or meaningful image which is more than the sum of its parts. For example, someone listening to a piece of music does not hear a series of individual notes but a melody.

This process of forming a gestalt was first discovered in the latter part of the nineteenth century by a group of German psychologists who observed human and animal behaviour in order to understand how man's perceptions of his environment influence his learning. Another important characteristic of perception, they discovered, is the individual's movement toward closure. A figure is seen as a complete bounded image – in some cases the perceiver even visually compensates for gaps in outline as, for example, in seeing these separate dots as the figure of a circle.

The psychologists also discovered that any incomplete gestalt represents an 'unfinished situation' that clamours for attention and interferes with the formation of any new gestalt. A simple example of this process is the person, some few hours before a dental appointment, who has difficulty in concentrating on any activity for a reasonable length of time. The emerging gestalt of the dental appointment blocks out all other 'gestalten' and he fails to deal satisfactorily with any other task.

Frederick S. Perls (1893-1970), now recognized as the founder of Gestalt therapy, began to apply these ideas in the field of psychotherapy in the 1940's. 'Fritz' Perls originally qualified as a doctor in Berlin in 1921. He was trained in psychoanalysis at the Psychoanalytical Institutes of Berlin, Frankfurt and Vienna. During his time at Frankfurt, Perls became acquainted with the work of the Gestalt laboratory psychologists, particularly Max Wertheimer and Wolfgang Kohler. Although he later described himself as 'not a pure Gestaltist'[1], Perls was particularly interested in the idea of the unfinished situation, the incomplete gestalt. Forced to flee Germany with his wife, he worked in private practice in Amsterdam in 1933–34, until the threat of Nazism made it necessary to emigrate to South Africa, where he became a training psychoanalyst, served as a psychiatrist for the British Army, and established the South Africa Institute for Psychoanalysis in 1935. In 1942 he published *Ego, Hunger and Aggression*[2], the first statement of the applications of the principles of Gestalt psychology to personality development and psychotherapeutic practice. In 1946 he moved to the United States where he worked in private practice and was psychiatrist in residence at Esalen Institute, Big Sur, California, where he conducted training workshops and seminars in Gestalt therapy from 1964 to 1969. The term 'Gestalt therapy' was first used as a title of a book on Perls' methods, written by him and two co-authors, Ralph Hefferline and Paul Goodman, in 1951[3]. Before his death Perls founded, or helped to establish, the Institute for Gestalt Therapy in New York, and similar institutes in Cleveland and San Francisco.

Gestalt therapy is based on the following assumptions about the nature of people[4]:

(1)   Each person is a whole who is (rather than has) a body, emotions, thoughts, sensations and perceptions – all of which function interrelatedly.
(2)   Each person is part of his/her environment and cannot be understood apart from it.
(3)   Each person is proactive rather than reactive, and determines his/her own responses to the world.
(4)   Each person is capable of being aware of his/her sensations, thoughts, emotions and perceptions.
(5)   Each person, through self-awareness, is capable of choice and is therefore responsible for own behaviour.
(6)   Each person possesses the potential and resources to live effectively and to satisfy own needs.
(7)   Each person can experience himself/herself only in the present. The past and the future can be experienced only in the now, through remembering and anticipating.
(8)   People are neither intrinsically good nor bad.

It can be seen that many of these assumptions are shared by other approaches derived from the general school of 'humanistic psychology', e.g. Transactional Analysis, T-groups, Encounter, Psychodrama, Bioenergetics etc. (For an outline of humanistic psychology, including details on some of these approaches *see* Shaffer[5]). In recent years there has been a growing recognition that these approaches can be applied in organizations for developing interpersonal skills and for organization development. The first major sign that this was happening with Gestalt therapy occurred in 1977 with the publication of *Authentic Management: a Gestalt orientation to organizations and their development*, by Stanley M. Herman and Michael Korenich[6]. This book, which covers methods, theories and exercises, also includes detailed case histories based on the authors' experiences in working with large organizations in the USA.

Our experiences at Roffey Park Management College over the last eight years suggest that the Gestalt approach is likely to help individuals (and organizations) who have problems with unproductive patterns of behaviour, e.g. dependency, compliance, unresolved conflict, lack of assertion and creativity etc. These, and similar repetitive patterns, yield little satisfaction to any of the parties involved and can lead to stultification within organizations. In terms of training we have found that the Gestalt approach is particularly effective in the following areas:

(1) Interpersonal skills training based on personal awareness (as used on our 'Interpersonal Relationships in Organizations' and 'Personal Awareness Development' programmes).
(2) Assertiveness and Influencing Skills (as used on our 'Personal Effectiveness and Power' programmes).
(3) Counselling (as used on our 'Personal Counselling in Organisations' programmes).
(4) Training of interpersonal skills trainers (as used on both our 'Methods of Interpersonal Skills Training' and 'Process Interventions Workshop' programmes).
(5) Team-building programmes.

How Gestalt is used on these programmes varies – in broad terms Chapter 6 describes how it is used on (1). The exercises described in Chapter 9 are used on (2)-(5), and each of these programmes includes some theoretical inputs as well as personal learning.

References

1. PERLS, Frederick S. *In and Out the Garbage Pail.* Bantam Books 1972.
2. PERLS, Frederick S. *Ego, Hunger and Aggression.* Vintage Books 1969.
3. PERLS, Frederick S., HEFFERLINE, R. F., and GOODMAN, P. *Gestalt Therapy.* Pelican 1973.
4. *Adapted from* p. 14 PASSONS, William R. *Gestalt Approaches in Counselling.* Holt, Rinehart & Winston, New York 1975.
5. SHAFFER, John B. P. *Humanistic Psychology.* Prentice-Hall 1978.
6. HERMAN, S. M. and KORENICH, M. *Authentic Management.* Addison-Wesley 1977.

CHAPTER 2

GESTALT FORMATION AND DESTRUCTION

The basic idea of the Gestalt approach is that personal needs arise and are satisfied in a pattern of gestalt formations and destructions. For example:

It is late evening and a man is sitting comfortably in an armchair reading an absorbing book in a centrally-heated home. Although he is not aware of it, the heating system switches off automatically and the room begins to cool. At this stage the book continues to hold his attention and forms the foreground or 'figure'; the cooling temperature is the background, or 'ground'. At first he is not aware of the drop in temperature, but gradually, as it becomes colder, he begins to respond to the change unconsciously. He tucks his legs beneath him and moves slightly in order to sit more compactly and retain body heat. His conscious attention, however, is still entirely in the book whilst his body begins to respond to another need. The gestalt, in relation to his need for warmth, is beginning to form, although it has not yet become 'figure'.

Gradually, as the temperature drops, his discomfort penetrates increasingly into his awareness. He makes additional efforts to ignore the cold and maintain his involvement with the book but there comes a point at which he can no longer sustain his interest in reading. At this point the existing need or interest is destroyed in favour of a new one – the need to maintain body comfort through warmth. The new gestalt emerges into and now occupies the centre of his attention. He leaves the book and the chair and takes some action designed to restore his comfort – he turns the heating back on.

Once he is warm again he can pick up the book and quickly the temperature, along with other possible concerns, becomes part of the ground, and the book's contents begin to absorb him again.

. . . .

Needs are present in a hierarchy so priorities resulting from the relationship between the individual and the environment are fulfilled to drop away and be replaced by other needs. The cycle of Gestalt formation and destruction is diagrammatically shown in Fig. 1 below.

Relating this model to the episode of the central heating it can be seen that the 'new situation' was prompted by a drop in room temperature. The 'need' for maintaining body warmth was signalled by 'awareness' of physical discomfort. The 'action' of turning the central heating on involved 'contact' with the switch and this led to 'satisfaction' of the need.

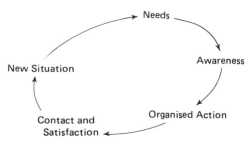

FIG. 1. Gestalt Formation and Destruction

All those but the mentally or physically sick and the poor or oppressed can orient and organize themselves sufficiently to satisfy their needs concerned with most physical functioning. The majority find breathing, eating, drinking, excreting and resting, fairly straightforward and satisfying, although this is not as obvious as it perhaps seems at first glance. People who eat too much, drink too much, suffer from constipation or insomnia are not thought of as sick, but for these people even basic physical functioning, let alone the more complex emotional and psychological needs, presents difficulties.

The emotional and psychological needs are more elusive. For example, the need to give and receive approval, love, recognition, companionship, stimulation, interest, acceptance and communication. In these circumstances the individual may have problems in perceiving his need clearly or may not know how to satisfy the need. When dealing with one or all of these needs his experience may be a sense of uneasiness or confusion.

An example in management might be an employee's uneasy feeling that his boss treats other members of his group of subordinates in a more relaxed, informal way. He may seem to talk with them frequently, freely and with warmth. But with this employee the boss is rather formal and more abrupt. The employee perhaps feels hurt and isolated and finds himself pulling back from contact both with the boss and his peers. This dissatisfaction leads to a sense of isolation, low motivation and a drop in work output which in itself produces a vicious circle. The employee tells himself there is nothing he can do: either he carries on as he is or he goes and finds another job.

Here the need for personal recognition and acceptance remains unsatisfied and being 'unfinished business' disturbs the healthy pattern of emerging needs and their satisfaction. In this way collections of unfinished business impede the individual so that he becomes less clear and less ready for the next experience.

In terms of the Gestalt model the ground can become over-crowded with urgent unsatisfied needs, each competing with each other for priority. Like a host of people trying to get through a narrow doorway at the same time few, if any, actually get through. The experience of having many unsatisfied needs clamouring for attention may be confusion, agitation, anxiety or difficulty in concentrating on one thing for the time it takes to deal with it. Each new event gives rise to a further piece of unfinished business, which adds to the profusion of dissatisfactions which obstruct the smooth flow of need fulfilment.

To ask for what is wanted or to express the feelings may well be enough to complete the gestalt. Alternatively, to find some more creative and new ways for satisfying the need elsewhere would leave the individual free to give all his attention to what would then become a new situation.

It takes courage to try out and experiment with new ways of behaving and new kinds of relationships, without knowing in advance what the result of the actions will be. A common example is asking someone to be a friend and risking their rejection. Many fear rejection so much that they never get round to asking!

This quality of courage and trust in the personal ability to survive, adapt and be satisfied is developed in Gestalt training through experience.

The process of healthy creative adaptation occurs moment by moment as the individual encounters the environment. It entails a sequence of events and experiences which begin with a sense of 'beneficial indifference'. A state of well-being and satisfaction in which he is ready for the next experience without any positive or negative interest in anything in particular. At this moment there is no figure, the ground is a fertile field in which some object of interest will grow. In the next moment from among a series of, until now, equally unimportant possibilities, some aspect begins to emerge as more significant. As he begins to recognize and endow this figure with interest, feeling and energy, it forms more and more clearly. As the figure emerges and brightens until it stands out clearly, he begins to approach or explore the environment, seeking out the means or possibility of need fulfilment. This process of orientation gives way to further activity in which he makes contact with the environment. In the course of this contact he changes the environment by adding, taking, exchanging, destroying, creating etc. As he does this he destroys the gestalt. The bright figure of interest dies away leaving the ground clear and he returns to a state of beneficial indifference — ready for something new.

This entire process can take place in the space of less than one second or may require minutes, hours, days or even years. At one level, turning down a car radio that is too loud, or perhaps adjusting the heater. At another level, stopping the car to eat a meal and at a third completing a project that has taken several weeks. In terms of communication or relationships it might mean one person making eye contact with a colleague and exchanging smiles, it might mean asking him for information. It might mean confronting the colleague about his lack of consideration. Each of these activities involves awareness, orientation, action, contact and completion.

CHAPTER 3

AWARENESS

The danger involved in talking about awareness is that the discussion contravenes a basic assumption in Gestalt about the nature of man. This assumption is:

> Man is a whole who *is* (rather than *has*) a body, emotions, thoughts, sensations and perceptions, all of which function interrelatedly.

An implication of this assumption is that emotions, thoughts and physical feelings are integrated experiences which it makes no sense to separate into abstractions such as mind and body. In terms of awareness, the only question to be answered is the starting point. Wherever awareness starts, with thoughts, feelings or physical sensation, the associated experiences in the other dimensions will be readily attended to.

For example, if someone is given a difficult mental exercise like a brain-teaser problem, it will not be long before he begins to tighten muscles perhaps in the jaw or the back of the neck and shoulders, and he begins to become restless and agitated. At the emotional level the individual is likely to feel frustrated and angry. In this process then physical, emotional and intellectual experiences are linked and it is hard to differentiate where one experience starts and another stops. The Gestalt approach encourages the integration of experience into a meaningful whole. The process of integration can begin with thoughts or fantasies, with physical sensations or with the emotions. Wherever the process starts the completion of a gestalt will involve all three types of energy.

In order to develop understanding, however, this chapter divides awareness into four different zones – emotions, thoughts, physical sensation and the external world.

Emotion

Awareness of self is central to the process of recognizing the needs that arise during the conduct of tasks and relationships. The guide to these needs are the emotions and feelings that are experienced. In simple terms anger is a guide to the wish to destroy or fight, sadness is concerned with loss, fear with the need to take flight or escape, pleasure with the wish to get more or move closer. At their strongest these feelings are unmistakable. Quickly, without thinking, these emotions instruct behaviour. The individual uses his energy to destroy or change what makes him angry, grieves for his loss, moves away from what is frightening and approaches or stays with what is pleasing.

Weaker emotional signals are less easily attended to or may be ignored and the guidance system breaks down. Holding back anger, even a little of it, leaves some need unsatisfied; putting a brave face on sadness leaves a need for comfort; ignoring fear results in insecurity; and neglecting pleasure leaves a sense of dissatisfaction. The effects of these emotional restraints are cumulative.

Continuing awareness of feelings and sensitivity to the feelings of others enables the individual to lead an exciting and satisfying life in which he is open to new possibilities and is ready for the next experience.

Lack of awareness of feelings in chronic form results in the collection of unfinished business and unsatisfied needs. The person who has learned to hide his needs for attention from others beneath a guise of indifference or cynicism is, at some level of awareness, still trying to satisfy those needs. Usually these emotional blind spots are in one or two particular areas – blocking perhaps anger, or sadness, or fear – rather than all feelings. The loss of awareness of some feelings then means the loss of a full functioning guidance system for action.

Being aware of feelings gives a sense of direction for action but in itself is not enough. The individual also needs to know how to be creative and adaptive in expressing them. The small infant initially uses very simple ways of getting what he wants – crying, smiling, grabbing, smashing. In growing up he learns new patterns of behaviour and to control and postpone some immediate wants in order for them to be better satisfied. In this way the family acts as a kind of emotional gymnasium in which are developed some muscles but not others. An individual's emotional development is therefore limited by his early experiences. Additionally, as he gets older many of his abilities decline with lack of use. Physical fitness is created from frequent and vigorous exercise and, whilst often painful at the time (with aches in muscles that he did not know he had) is recognized as being healthy.

The same process applies to feelings and the Gestalt approach encourages the expression of emotions as a means for dealing with present needs and, in specific exercises, as a means for developing emotional fitness. Just as physical fitness does not imply physical violence so emotional fitness does not lead to the excessive or inappropriate use of feelings, but to their sensitive and effective expression. The Gestalt training ground then acts as a continuation of the emotional gymnasium where, under supervision, people can undertake exercises which stretch and stimulate, bringing about flexibility, strength and stamina.

Thought

Because of the importance attached to emotion in the Gestalt approach the process of thinking (theorizing, remembering, anticipating, explaining, imagining, guessing, comparing, planning etc) is often seen as an interruption to the awareness of feeling. A person may use thinking as a block to awareness of emotions, turning inward on himself and breaking contact with others. Thinking activity is a form of 'fantasy', i.e. dealing with what is not here or now, and can be used as a way of limiting contact with others. When a person starts thinking, the Gestalt approach may focus the individual on his process of switching from action into thinking, or encourage him to say his thoughts out loud. For example, people often 'rehearse' in their heads what they are going to say or do before the event. By giving voice to these rehearsals the individual becomes more aware of the choices he gives himself and, more importantly, the choices he denies himself. Explanations are often offered as substitutes for action. For example, the individual recognizing that he is afraid to express appreciation of what someone else has done is an important first step in the process of need fulfilment, but in itself it does not satisfy the need to give the appreciation. It is by discovering directly that what he learned earlier in life can be modified or abandoned, *now in this context*, that he can begin to fulfil his needs and make new choices.

Similarly, interpretations are not considered a useful way of understanding others. An interpretation is an attempt by one person to rationalize, explain or label the behaviour of another. There are three problems with interpretations. One, the interpretation may be wrong and therefore denies the recipient's experience of himself. Two, the person may accept the interpretation as a boundary and may lose the possibility of discovering new creative and satisfying ways of meeting their needs. Three, others may respond to the person on the basis of the interpretation, e.g. 'John is being defensive again'.

The emphasis of Gestalt on learning by discovery from direct experience makes it exciting and sometimes confronting and painful. The relegation of intellectual understanding below action, contact and satisfaction can be at odds with the cultural values of our society. The educational system is geared to intellectual understanding, and organizations employ staff largely because of their capacity to think and to make sense of the environment. Thinking is a basic means for solving problems, managing machines, understanding and predicting events, and other essential functions for staying alive and saving a lot of unnecessary trouble and effort. In relationships, however, thinking can get in the way. One of the reasons that it can do so is because many people try to make a clear distinction between emotion and thinking. Man is not a computer – understanding, explaining, interpreting, remembering, anticipating, guessing, comparing, planning etc are all based on experience and are shaped by the context in which they occur, and therefore each of these activities has some emotional quality. When the individual thinks, he may lose awareness of his feelings but he does not stop feeling. In these terms, the exclusively rational organization is a myth.

There is a further paradox for organizations which expect members of staff to repress their feelings. Gestalt encourages awareness of feelings and their expression because feelings can lead to individual creativity in all aspects of living. Therefore, organizational standards of behaviour which discourage feelings also restrict the opportunities for individual and group creativity. The consequences for the organization can be rigidity, inflexibility, and therefore an inability to cope with changing circumstances.

Physical Sensation

The third starting point is the awareness of what goes on inside the body, what can be felt on the surface and from inside the skin — itches, muscular tensions and movements, physical manifestations of feelings and emotions, discomfort, well-being etc. From an early age people learn a variety of controls for hiding their feelings — each of these mechanisms involves some form of muscle control or tension. A simple example of this can be found when an individual forces himself to smile. As he maintains the smile he quickly becomes aware of the rigidity and tension in his lower facial muscles. When an individual habitually represses a particular emotion the resulting physical tension, although often intense, is likely to be outside his awareness. This form of repression can induce psychosomatic illnesses.

These physical signs of tension are powerful cues that an event of some significance is happening inside the individual. Some common examples of these clues are:

1. Breathing irregularities such as catching breath, sighing, blowing out, holding breath, shallow breathing. (It is a unique contribution of the Gestalt approach to provide a link between the physical, emotional and mental experiences. The key to this link is the most basic form of relationship between an individual and the environment — breathing. An interruption of the normal breathing pattern is an interruption of contact with the environment. It is a part of the process of interrupting the normal flow of interest, creative adaptation and need fulfilment. These breathing interruptions can be momentary such as controlled breathing in the upper chest. The breathing interruption is not just an indication of a block in the cycle of need fulfilment, it *is* in itself a part of the block. Releasing the restricted control over breathing leads to the possibility of completion. The internal experience of the breathing interruption is what Gestalt calls anxiety, the gap between now and then. Anxiety is the result of blocking the cycle of need fulfilment by restricting the chest, so that it cannot cope with the increase in breathing required to support the excitement of discovery. Therefore, anxiety, interruption of breathing and the

disruption of the forming gestalt are all three different facets of a single process.)

2. Swallowing, clearing the throat, coughing, constricting the throat. (These signals often demonstrate the tensions arising from attempting to keep down what the individual finds difficult to say.)

3. Muscle-tightening jaw or fist-clenching, pressing or pushing down, curling up fingers or toes. Stretching or distorting face, fixed smile, frowning, furrowing brows. (These signals often illustrate the using up of energy which could be used to make contact with others.)

4. Agitation, foot-finger-hand-tapping, holding a part of the self. (Often a clue that an individual is holding on to some unexpressed emotion.)

5. Low voice, unnatural rigidity of posture and absence of movement. (Often a clue that the individual is repressing all energy, is trying to fade into the background.)

6. Blinking, closing eyes, looking away, up, down. (Often a clue that the individual is trying to avoid contact with others.)

7. Stroking or rubbing hands, legs, face, arms or neck. (Often a clue that the individual is needing comfort from others or wants to give comfort to others.)

It is important to say that the physical behaviours and the suggested interpretations do not always indicate the same internal processes. When dealing with these behaviours, there is a need to consider the context in which they occur, i.e. what else is happening.

Although these physical activities may be momentary they provide information for the individual concerned and others that some relevant internal process is taking place. Among the ways of exploring these further are:

1. Awareness — pay attention to the behaviour.

2. Identification — identify more closely with the experience: 'What do you experience as you tap your fingers on the chair?'.

3. Exaggeration — exaggerate the behaviour.

4. Stop — use energy in a more purposeful way: 'Make contact with someone in the room'.

External World

The final area is awareness of the external world. In particular, awareness of the expressed feelings, spoken thoughts, the physical movements of others. Also awareness of objects and events — what can be seen, heard, smelt, tasted or touched. By paying attention to such objects and events the individual can become aware of his own emotional responses — however light — to these stimuli, e.g. enjoying, rather than merely drinking, a cup of coffee; disliking the shape of a chair etc.

A basic assumption in the Gestalt approach is that the external world, the environment, is the source of satisfaction for all the individual's needs through the contact boundary. Therefore, clear awareness of the external world is a prerequisite for ensuring that needs can be satisfied (e.g. the individual being able to identify who is more likely to offer him support, concern, honesty, love, fun, excitement etc). This ability to be aware of others, recognizing the cues that they offer – and these cues may range from clear statements, e.g. 'I trust you' to fairly subtle non-verbal behaviours, e.g. attentive eye contact – requires the individual to pay attention to the evidence derived from all his senses (sight, sound, touch, taste, smell). This process of testing reality – noticing what is available – can be impaired by the individual either not using all the information available to him or by distorting the information to match a preconception. An illustration of how this can occur is provided by the episode of a new member of staff who is asked by his boss to prepare and submit a report to the next meeting of the departmental management team. The new member of staff works slavishly on the report because he sees it as a major opportunity to impress both his boss and his colleagues. During his presentation at the meeting he notices two members whispering together. Because of his concern to impress he views their behaviour as, at best, discourteous and, at worst, a prelude to being attacked by them when he finishes. At this point he focuses all his attention on them and excludes all other members. In reality, however, the pair are sharing their appreciations of his report and, because of his concern, the new member of staff does not notice the approving glances from the other members of the team.

In any relationship this process of selective perception may be used by both parties and the contact between them is likely to be based more on assumption than on reality. Where this occurs both use their awareness of the other to confirm their assumptions, e.g. certain statements are ignored or misunderstood; an even tone of voice may be experienced as aggression; eye contact as menacing; body posture as threatening; silence as intimidation, etc. The internal processes which interrupt contact with others and shape selective perception are described in the next chapter.

CHAPTER 4

INTERRUPTIONS

The Gestalt approach is directly concerned with the ways people interrupt their contact with the environment and avoid the possibility of satisfying their needs at any one time. These interruptions are learned patterns of behaviour which made sense at some stage in their lives — usually in the early relationship between the child and his parents — but now are often inappropriate in relationships with others. For example, a child may quickly learn that whenever he makes some demand on his parents for their attention he will be punished in some way, e.g. told to be quiet, smacked, sent out of the room. He therefore learns that the way to get their approval is to be undemanding, unobtrusive, have the ability to fade into the background. Having made the adjustment he habitually uses these skills in his adult life when he deals with 'parent' figures, like a senior manager. His experience is used to shape his view of himself and of the world that he deals with. One of the consequences of repeating these learned patterns of behaviour is to re-affirm the individual's view of the world and to keep it predictable and safe.

There are five types of interruption — introjection, projection, confluence, retroflection and deflection. Before looking in detail at these interruptions it will be useful to describe some aspects of contact.

Interruptions are momentary and normally unnoticed by the individual in whom they occur. An observer's clue to interruptions are the myriad of physical events that take place in the body and above all breathing interruptions or irregularities. They can be brought into awareness and used as a guide to need fulfilment by deliberately attending to them and by receiving feedback.

A major assumption in Gestalt is that the individual is dependent on the environment for the satisfaction of all his needs. A simple example of this is the need to breathe. In order to breathe the individual needs to take in oxygen from the environment. Therefore, to understand the individual there is a need to look at the way he makes contact (which involves sensing, feeling, assimilating, rejecting, touching, conflicting etc) with his environment. The place at which he makes contact is called the contact boundary. The ability of an individual to make effective contact with his environment and satisfy his needs at any time depends on his awareness of his own boundary (Who am I here and now?) and awareness of the environment (Where am I here and now?).

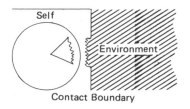

FIG. 2. Introjection

From birth the individual is confronted by a range of rules and standards of behaviour. These rules and standards represent demands being made on him by the environment. Apart from rejecting or ignoring them there are two ways of dealing with these demands. The first response is assimilation – which involves selecting out of the mass those rules which can be accepted and absorbed as part of the self because they make sense to the individual concerned. The second response is introjection – which involves swallowing down a set of rules and standards either because someone has told the person to do so, and reinforced their statement by punishment and/or reward, or because they are fashionable or safe or traditional, or dangerous or revolutionary. These undigested attitudes, ways of acting, feeling and evaluating are called introjects. As Fig. 2 shows, this process involves giving up part of the self to accommodate part of the environment.

Organizations are maintained with rules, standards and attitudes that restrict behaviour which can be swallowed whole as introjects. For example, an employee being told by a colleague that training courses are used by management as a way of punishing people. When a manager makes a statement beginning, 'We have always done this . . .', or, 'We have no choice . . .', then he is likely to be responding to an introject.

Introjects give rise to two types of problems: first, the person who introjects limits his choices of behaviour with rules which are often irrelevant and which get in the way of the process of need satisfaction. Second, it is possible to swallow potentially conflicting introjects ('Be nice to people' and 'Don't show your feelings') and to be torn apart in the process of trying to reconcile them.

When an individual discards an introject he is then able to enjoy the freedom to set standards that make sense for him and which do not get in the way of the process of need satisfaction. For example, the person who discards the introject 'Don't get close to people', can begin the process of discrimination in his relationships. He can discover for the first time that his needs for friendship and closeness can be satisfied by different people in a variety of ways.

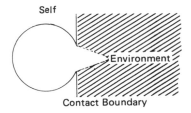

FIG. 3. Projection

As introjection is the tendency to make the self a host for what actually is part of the environment, so projection is the tendency to make the environment a host for what originates in the self. An extreme case of projection can be found in the paranoiac – his conviction that he is being persecuted is better understood as a statement of his desire to persecute others. Examples of more common occurrence are the manipulative subordinate who complains that his boss can not be trusted; or, the cold, haughty, withdrawn manager who accuses colleagues of being unfriendly to him.

The projector's assumption about the other may well be founded on some reality of observable behaviour. The cold, haughty, withdrawn manager is likely to meet many people who behave coldly to him.

It is also possible for the individual to use this mechanism on himself. For the projector has a tendency not only to disown his own impulses, but also to disown those parts of himself in which the impulses arise. He gives them, as it were, an objective existence outside himself, so that he can avoid responsibility both for his troubles and that they originate with him. The man who complains after a meeting, 'All this talking has given me a headache', neatly side-steps the responsibility of giving himself a headache by passing it on to that part of him who does the talking!

By 'owning' projections the individual begins to take responsibility for those discarded parts of himself, e.g. coldness, desire to persecute. Although at first sight such qualities may appear to be undesirable, the reality is that coldness or the desire to persecute are not intrinsically bad. The real issue is their appropriateness or inappropriateness in any situation. Until the individual owns to these particular feelings then he is unable to discriminate whether their opposites, warmth and the desire to care for, are also appropriate in any situation. The growth of an individual is viewed in Gestalt terms as a continuing process of integration. Also, by owning projections the individual learns to recognize and appreciate the uniqueness of each individual that he encounters.

Self

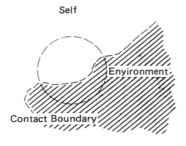

FIG. 4. Confluence

When the individual feels no boundary at all between himself and his environment, when he feels that he and it are one, then he is in a state of confluence. By failing to distinguish between the boundaries of self and the environment — as shown in Fig. 4 — then the individual operates from a kind of emotional colour-blindness. Newborn infants live in confluence, they have no sense of any distinction between inside and outside, between the self and other. The man who is in pathological confluence ties up his needs, his emotions and his activities in one bundle of utter confusion until he is no longer aware of what he wants to do and how he is preventing himself from doing it. A more common occurrence of confluence is the person who absurdly identifies himself with another person — protesting, in spite of all contradictory evidence that they are exactly alike. The contradictory evidence is either ignored or dismissed by the individual. Some organizations actively promote confluence by demanding a strong, but narrow, sense of loyalty from their employees. A form of loyalty which requires unthinking identification with the management view and the avoidance of all forms of conflict breeds corporate confluence. The consequences to the organization are loss of creativity and an inability to respond to a changing business environment.

As the individual learns to see through his confluence he becomes aware of who he is and what he wants. He is able to value himself not because he is the same as others, but because he is unique. He also learns to value the uniqueness of others. One of the rewards of working through confluence is to experience the excitement of discovery and, in the words of Louis Macneice, to feel 'The drunkenness of things being various.'

To retroflect literally means 'to turn back sharply against'. When a person retroflects behaviour he treats himself as he originally wanted to treat other persons or objects. He stops directing his energies outward in attempts to mani-

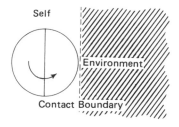

FIG. 5. Retroflection

pulate and bring about changes in his environment that will satisfy his needs: instead he re-directs his activity inwards and substitutes himself in place of his environment as the target for his behaviour. To the extent that he does this he splits his personality into doer and done to. He can literally become his own worst enemy. As Fig. 5 shows, this process involves the individual creating a boundary within himself. The person who feels angry with another but refuses to express it turns the anger inward and punishes himself with feelings of guilt, sadness, inadequacy etc. This process is often signalled by furrowed brows, muscular tension or stiffness and the frequent use of the word 'myself'. Similarly, the person who is unable or reluctant to seek comfort from others will comfort himself by stroking his own arm or leg. The retroflector makes statements like: 'I am ashamed of myself', or, 'I have to force myself to do this job'. All statements of this sort are based on the surprising conception that he and himself are two different people. When people leave meetings and complain about being bored or criticizing the behaviour of the autocratic chairman they are likely to have spent much of their time at the meeting retroflecting.

When an individual stops retroflecting and turns his energy outwards onto the environment, he may be faced with his own catastrophic fantasy. For example, the person who normally retroflects anger may have the fantasy that, were he to express the feeling the recipient would be severely damaged in some way. Similarly, the individual who retroflects his need for comfort may have the fantasy that the recipient will ostracise him or hurt him in some cruel way. When the retroflector does take the risk and, at the time, it is felt to be a major risk, he is likely to discover that the catastrophe does not occur. The usual, though not universal, consequence of sharing feelings is that the relationship becomes closer and more rewarding. Similarly, the consequence for the initiator is an increased confidence in being who he is.

Deflection, as shown in Fig. 6, involves the individual acting as if he was operating behind a deflection screen, moving away from the possibility of satisfying a need.

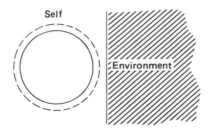

FIG. 6. Deflection

These deflections can take many forms:

taking the heat out of a situation (e.g. 'There is no reason to be upset');
laughing off an uncomfortable situation or experience;
being abstract or polite;
minimizing an emotion or need (e.g. 'It's not important');
talking about the possibility of being upset or angry rather than acknowledging that you are;
being diplomatic (e.g. 'I think we need to move on');
grandiosity (e.g. 'I am a failure');
denying emotions (e.g. 'We need to be rational and adult about this').

To move from deflection to full contact is to experience the difference between distance and involvement and to be open to the possibility that raising the conflict, rather than avoidance, is more likely to lead to both parties achieving satisfaction.

Although it is possible to distinguish between and to describe the five different types of interruption, it is important to say that they rarely occur in isolation. An individual is likely to compound the process of interrupting the cycle of need fulfilment, for example, with combinations of introjects ('I must not show my feelings'), retroflection (clenching the jaw to hold back anger), and confluence (failing to notice his own actions). Whatever the combinations one feature of confluence is that it is always present as a secondary state to the other interruptions.

CHAPTER 5

GESTALT TRAINING

This chapter describes the characteristics of a Gestalt training group and the type of activities that are likely to take place. Before doing this there are three general points that need to be mentioned: one, the relationship between training and therapy; two, the Gestalt view of the nature of personal change; and, three, arising out of the second point, the trainer encouraging and giving permission to people to 'be' rather than 'do' in the group.

Training and Therapy

Gestalt therapy was developed by Perls as an alternative to Freudian psycho-analysis, to be practised on either a long-term or short-term basis with clients. But arising from the time Perls spent at the Esalen Institute, and his practice there of running short-term courses for people who wanted to learn more about themselves, Gestalt has also developed as a 'therapy' for ordinary people — part of the wider movement of humanistic psychology. Two important characteristics of humanistic psychology are:

1. People have considerable potential for growth, and generally a lot more than they realize.
2. There are no right answers. Each person, who is by definition unique, can find his own path to self-fulfilment.

Because interpersonal skills trainers have liberally borrowed approaches and techniques from the rich field of humanistic psychology (Maslow, Transactional Analysis, Encounter etc. as well as Gestalt) over the last twenty years, there has consequently been an erosion of the boundary between training and therapy. Although it can be argued that training and therapy have more similarities than differences, the Gestalt trainer needs to be clear in his own mind about the distinctions that can be observed. For example, not encouraging people to re-experience historic family issues; dealing with concerns that arise from their involvement in organizational life; to operate with the humanistic psychology model (i.e. people have the potential for growth) rather than the 'medical' model (man the 'sick animal') used by some therapists; having the ability to recognize the limits of their competence in working with any individual.

Nature of Personal Change

The Gestalt view of the nature of personal change can be summarized in the paradoxical statement:

> The individual grows by becoming more of what he *is* rather than by trying to be *different*.

This means that the individual cannot be other than what it is his nature to be, and that any attempts by him, or others on him, to change are destined to failure. This is an important issue in Gestalt groups because people often approach the event with a 'programme' of change mapped out for themselves. Such a 'programme' is likely to arise from a sense of personal dissatisfaction ('I must not be arrogant') or because the individual has received feedback from colleagues ('I want you to stop being arrogant'). The usual consequence for the individual in such circumstances is to put himself under tremendous pressure, and to feel uncomfortable and unhappy.

Permission to Be

All of the activities that take place in Gestalt groups have the explicit intention of helping individuals to be more of who they are. Discovery is therefore dependent on the individual's willingness to engage in some activity with the trainer or other group members. In addition to this process of discovery there is an equally important dimension in the group – the individual receiving permission to be who he is. For example, having permission to take part in an activity or not; to leave the room or not. Similarly, having permission to be angry, sad, jealous, scornful, tearful or happy. The permission to be is a powerful injunction for the group member who has a 'programme'. When he tells the trainer that he wants to learn how not to be arrogant, for example, he is likely to receive the response: 'It's O.K. to be arrogant here', or, 'I would like to see your arrogance'. The permission offers relief from the self-induced pressure to change and allows the participant self-acceptance and the chance to value himself as he is rather than as he imagines he should be.

The Training Group

The normal setting for Gestalt training is a small group of, say, 6-12 participants under the direction of trained leadership. The group forms a social environment within which individuals develop awareness of themselves and others. Although the group is an important feature of the training it seems, initially, to have a fairly limited role in the learning process. Because of the strong individual focus of the Gestalt approach much of the explicit interaction in the group is between the trainer and a single participant. When someone is in the 'hot seat' the group may be asked to refrain from contributing until the piece of work is finished. Then they are asked to share whatever they wish about their experiences and reactions (particularly their feelings) during the course of the work. This feedback is an important source of both group interaction and support for it demonstrates that others relate to and identify with the participant who is working with the trainer. In the process they identify unfinished business for themselves. Another important role for the group during work is to act as audience and/or participants in any exercises or experiments with behaviour which are offered by the trainer to the individual.

Either explicitly at the start of a group, or gradually over a period of time, certain ground rules are introduced by the trainer. These ground rules are intended to set the appropriate conditions for personal experimentation by confronting many of the accepted patterns of interpersonal behaviour. They are not intended as 'musts' or 'shoulds'. Following the ground rules in a mechanical way, or dutifully playing 'good trainee', is a negation of the Gestalt approach.

Ground Rules

1. *'Here and Now' Experience*

   In common with other approaches to interpersonal skills training, course members are asked to pay attention to their own feelings, sensations and behaviours as they occur. The purpose of this rule is to develop awareness, since it is awareness which provides the raw material for self-development. Paying attention to events such as breathing, tensions, self-stroking, avoiding contact, excitement, interest, memories, images, irritation, rejection, provides the individual with valuable information about who he is and what he wants at the moment. Talking about the past, present, or future results in little contact with others.

2. *Personal Responsibility*

   Every thought, feeling, statement, action is an expression of the person's identity at the moment. So course members are asked to 'own' or identify with what they are saying or doing. Many people have learnt to say 'one', 'we', 'people' or 'you' when they really mean 'I'; and 'can't' when they mean 'won't'. The response 'You can't go round saying that sort of thing', is a typical example.

   The clearer statement would be 'I won't say that'. The 'you' is changed to 'I' since the individual is actually talking about the prospect of his own actions, and the 'can't' is changed to 'won't' since the suggestion (for example, telling each member of the group something about them which he finds attractive) clearly is feasible and the issue is the person's willingness rather than ability. This ground rule serves to highlight confluence and projections in substituting 'I' for 'we' or 'people'. Each individual is encouraged to speak for himself, or at least to check with each member of the group about their experience to see if he is saying something that others agree with.

3. *Questions*

'Why' questions are generally discouraged for they invite individuals to 'talk about' instead of making contact and learning. In responding to such a question, e.g. 'Why are you silent?', an individual is capable of producing any number of plausible reasons, e.g. 'I'm always silent in groups', 'I have nothing to say' etc, and be no nearer to understanding who he is. For each of these responses begs another question, e.g. 'Why are you always silent in groups?', and so on and so on. By following such questions the individual ends up in the labyrinth of introspection. Often the 'why' question is an invitation for a person to explain, defend, or justify some aspect of himself or his existence. For example, 'Why did you say that to Alan?' may conceal the statement: 'I did not like what you said'. For this reason the trainer may invite a questioner to check out if there is a statement behind his question.

Developing awareness involves exploring the 'whats' and 'hows' of behaviour. So Gestalt trainers will make frequent interventions in the group by asking questions like, 'What are you doing now?' (to someone who has stopped speaking, for instance) and, 'How do you make yourself angry/scared/sad etc?'.

4. *Being Specific*

When speaking to each other, course members are encouraged to be direct, using the words 'I' and 'you' in their statements, e.g. 'I don't trust you'. Only in this way can they begin to explore and make contact with each other. In addition to taking responsibility for his actions the course member is identifying directly with those parts of himself he may be projecting onto others. In the example above the speaker may be saying more about his lack of trust in himself than about the recipient of the feedback. Similarly, the simple expedient of changing all 'it' statements into specific terms enables the individual to develop increased awareness of his own experiences. To say 'I feel cold now' instead of 'It is cold now' brings him closer to his experience. The use of the word 'it' applied to self and others is one way to keep distant from the experience.

5. *Simple Statements*

Course members are asked to describe their experiences in the simplest terms — 'I feel lonely', 'My head aches', 'I am confused'. Feelings and sensations are essentially simple experiences. Elaborate statements are often distorted with explanations or avoidance. For example, the statement 'I sort of feel unhappy . . . sometimes . . . it is most unusual', probably means 'I feel sad'.

6. *Interpretation*

As mentioned in Chapter 2, interpreting behaviour can be more hindering than helpful. When a person makes a statement about how he responds to the behaviour of another that is self-expression. When he interprets the meaning of another's behaviour that statement implies that the speaker knows what is motivating the other — which is fantasy. Most interpretations are based on projections — even if they are confirmed to be correct by the person on the receiving end — and say as much about the speaker as the receiver. The person who says to another course member 'I guess you had a tough time as a child', is likely to be asked by the trainer if that is also a statement about himself. The usual practice in Gestalt groups is to clearly prefix an interpretation with the words 'I guess that . . .' or 'I imagine that . . .'.

The ground rules, together with appropriate accommodation and a timetable, are the main structural elements of a training event. There are few other constraints with work proceeding as needs arise for individuals who find themselves unable to complete some gestalt. The trainer works with the individual to explore the 'blocks' or interruptions. The process is one of discovering unfinished business and building the self-support (through breathing and reality testing) necessary to let go of the block, integrating the split, making contact and closing the cycle. The role of the trainer is to be available to members of the group. One useful guideline for people attending a Gestalt group is to ensure that they do not take away more unfinished business than they arrived with. To this end the trainer is likely to start the event by inviting people in the group to state their wants and needs from the programme. Additionally, the last session of the event is likely to be clearly designated as an opportunity for people to finish up their outstanding concerns.

Ways of Working

The Gestalt approach is *not* a set of techniques or formulae for discovering self or others; it is an orientation to experience which is dynamic and flexible in which the individual is open to all possibilities. The process of creative adaptation is a way of being oriented toward the satisfaction of personal needs. There are therefore endless variations the trainer and trainee may use in the process of creative adaptation. Some of the common methods which are outlined below are used as starting points for growth. Some are not exclusive to Gestalt.

Continuum of Awareness

The continuum of awareness seems to be very simple, just to be aware from second to second of what is happening. Unless people are asleep they are always aware of something. However, as soon as this awareness becomes unpleasant, most people will interrupt it. They will interrupt by being anxious and intellectualizing, avoiding, confusing themselves, going blank, remembering the past, anticipating the future, or jumping from experience to experience like a grasshopper. When a course member is asked to describe what he is aware of now, the trainer will focus on the interruptions or the ways in which the course member limits his awareness. For example, if the person's awareness is limited to external events (someone speaking or moving, noise outside the room, the clock ticking etc) the trainer may ask him to focus on bodily sensations (aches, tensions, posture etc) and explore what happens as he interrupts this process.

Two-chair Work

With two-chair work an individual explores his internal splits by acting out a dialogue between two (or more) chairs which represent the conflicting elements. Often the dialogue is between one part expressing a 'should' and the other a 'want'. For example, the person who has learnt to repress his anger may enter into a dialogue between that part of him that forbids and another part which wishes to express the anger.

These types of dialogue are described as topdog-underdog conflicts. The topdog is usually righteous and authoritarian: he knows best. He is sometimes right, but always righteous. The topdog is a bully, and says things like 'You should' and 'You should not'. He manipulates and threatens with statements like − 'If you don't, then − you won't be loved, you will be rejected, you will be ashamed', and so on. The underdog, meanwhile, manipulates with being defensive, apologetic, whining and playing the victim. He replies with statements like 'I try my best', 'I can't help it if I fail', 'Leave me alone' etc. The underdog is cunning and usually gets the better of the topdog.

With two-chair work the individual clarifies the conflicting parts, identifies projections, introjects, expresses retroflections and by exploring them moves towards some new insight or creative adaptation which is likely to result in integration and completion.

Making Contact

This involves the course member making some kind of contact with the other members of the group. The trainer may invite him to make a specific statement to some, or all, of the other members in the group. By making the same statement to each person, the meaning of that statement can become focused in the centre of the person's awareness. For example, a person may feel at ease expressing anger and resentment but be unwilling to express warmth and affection. He might then be invited to find some way of expressing warmth and affection to others in the group. The success of such experiments will be validated by the individual's feelings about himself during and after the exercise. If he feels more relaxed, complete, or satisfied then the experiment has been successful. If he feels bad in some way – ashamed, scared etc – then he can explore these feelings with the trainer, probably via two-chair work, to identify the introjects that underpin the retroflection. Another way to make the rounds is for the individual to use the group for practising a new behaviour. For example, the person who has had no experience of openly criticizing others may be invited to go to each individual in turn to find as many ways as possible of expressing criticism, e.g. straight statement, sneering, making a sound that expresses criticism etc.

Dreams and Imagery

In Gestalt, dreams and images are viewed as statements of the concerns or the unfinished business of the individual and in a sense can be understood as retroflections or projections. The person is asked to bring his dream into the present by telling it aloud as if he is describing a film or play which he can see and the group cannot. Every detail of the dream is his own creation. He creates all the people, all the things, all the places, all the actions in his dream and they all reflect something of himself. The person is usually asked to focus on one or a few aspects of the dream that he is particularly interested in. He is then asked to describe the dream as if it were happening now. For example, if the person in describing the dream talks about walking down a country path he may be asked to 'Be the path – tell me what you look like'. The results of such explorations are exciting, dramatic, and effective because in the process of working on the dream the individual by-passes many of the blocks and resistances which he may use in other learning situations.

Similarly, when someone in talking about themselves uses an interesting image or metaphor, e.g. 'I feel as cold as ice', the trainer may offer the invitation 'Be the ice – describe yourself to me'. Exploring images in this way is often a powerful method for understanding oneself.

Drawings

One structured experience which a trainer might use, which offers similar possibilities to work on dreams and images, is to invite course members to draw a picture. The subject of the picture may be deliberately autobiographical, e.g. Life Portrait, or may be less directly personal, e.g. A Picture of Your Favourite Garden. The pictures are used in the same way as dreams or images. Often the most significant parts of the drawing are those which are seen initially by the artist as being unimportant, or those parts which are mentioned or suggested in the verbal description but are not shown in the drawing (e.g. a wall that contains the garden). For example, one man who drew a very complex and detailed Life Portrait worked avidly on all the images except for a last-minute addition to his drawing – the figure of an old woman. When he finally, and reluctantly, explored this image he began to work on the most important issue (as he later expressed) currently facing him at work. The image represented his view of his boss who he literally saw as an 'old woman'.

Be an Object

A similar intervention to drawings is to invite someone to select an object that interests him and to describe himself as that object, e.g. 'I am a Rolls Royce motor car; I am big, powerful and expensive etc'.

The Results of Training

The simple purpose of Gestalt training is to develop awareness of what is happening inside the trainee, and in his relationships with others, and to increase his ability to deal with what *is* rather than what ought to be or what might be. The task is not easy. The results can be disturbing and uncomfortable and the programme requires the guidance of an experienced trainer.

To be a trainee and to learn does not require any understanding of the theory of Gestalt. However, the effective integration of the learning is more likely when the trainee is able later to reflect on his experience with some cognitive understanding of what has taken place.

At worst a trainee will become more entrenched in self-limiting patterns of behaviour and will continue to see others as the cause of his problems, or continue to blame himself for the difficulties that the environment presents.

At best the trainee may discover how he limits himself; he will be able to review the rules which govern his life; he will realize how he has been imagining things about others and acting upon unreal perceptions; he will understand how he has shied away from openness and directness with himself and others, he will be able to see the differences between himself and others; he will have a wider repertoire of behaviour, be more flexible, less manipulative, more willing to assert himself or engage in conflicts. He will be more creative and enthusiastic by looking for and finding ways of being satisfied rather than waiting for things to go wrong and saying 'I told you so'. In short, a successful trainee will take responsibility for his own life and continue to discover ways of satisfying his needs by creative adaptation.

CHAPTER 6

TRANSCRIPTS

The following transcripts are from training programmes run at Roffey Park Management College. The only editing has been of repetitions to make them suitable for publication. We have changed the names of course members and are very grateful to the individuals concerned for giving us permission to publish the material.

I

At the beginning of this exchange Terry is reluctant to explore his expressed feeling of superiority to others in the group. By working with one of his images — a room — he was able to discover some unfinished business.

Trainer: In what ways do you feel superior now?
Terry: I am aware of stereotyping people . . . keeping myself above them . . . feeling critical of them.
Trainer: Are you prepared to share your criticisms?
Terry: I don't know if I want to.
Trainer: What would happen if you do?
Terry: I would feel superior to them . . . I can't think . . .
Trainer: What would happen if you lost your superiority?
Terry: I am not altogether sure that it is superiority. I'm beginning to withdraw from the group . . . I don't feel superior now . . .
(As he says this he slowly edges his chair back towards the door.)
Trainer: Are you aware of physically moving back?
Terry: I'm aware of doing that . . . I feel blank at the moment . . . I want to fade into the room.
Trainer: O.K., I would like you to close your eyes and describe yourself as this room. Start, 'I am a room . . .'.
Terry: (very fast) I am a room, four walls, roof, carpet, long window, flip-chart, nine people.
Trainer: I suggest you take your time and go through your description and see if anything interests you.
Terry: The walls are cream in colour.
Trainer: Say, 'I am cream coloured . . .'
Terry: I am cream coloured . . . I've got nine people sitting on me . . . (with this statement his voice is slow and laboured).
Trainer: Say that again.

Terry: I've got nine people sitting on me.
Trainer: What does it feel like having nine people sitting on you?
Terry: Very heavy... I feel heavy... I want to fall asleep. There is a fairly
            tense atmosphere in me... I'm aware of eight people looking at
            me... My eyelids are very heavy... I want to open my eyes.
Trainer: Where in your body do you feel tense?
Terry: Across my eyes. I want to open my eyes.
Trainer: How are you stopping yourself?
Terry: I can't... I'm getting very, very confused.
Trainer: Are you back in your room?
Terry: (No answer).
Trainer: Are you back in your room? (shouted)
Terry: Yes. (Opens eyes).
Trainer: I would like you to say to different individuals in the room, 'You are
            sitting on me and making me feel heavy'.

Terry completes the exercise and identifies three people in the room who he
uses to make himself feel heavy. He then describes some connection – their
eyes – between these three people and his father with whom he continues to
have a difficult relationship.

II

In this excerpt Steve has identified an issue which is creating problems in his
relationships with senior managers at work.

Steve: I want to work on the issue of how I make myself tense when dealing
            with people I respect or fear.
Trainer: Are you feeling tense now?
Steve: Yes.
Trainer: Where do you experience the tension?
Steve: Here (pointing to abdomen).
Trainer: I want you to describe yourself as the feeling of tension.
Steve: I am a spring inside Steve... keeping him down.
Trainer: Say that again.
Steve: I am keeping him down (slow solemn voice).
Trainer: How long have you been inside Steve?
Steve: (Slowly begins to smile, obviously pleased with his discovery). Since
            he was 12.
Trainer: What happened when you were 12 Steve?
Steve: I started fighting back against my elder brother who used to bully me.
Trainer: Do you want to finish up with your brother now?
Steve: Yes.

Steve is invited to do some two-chair work: from one chair Steve talks to his brother, he then switches chairs and continues the dialogue as his brother. The subsequent topdog-underdog conflict clarifies how Steve now avoids conflicts with others because of his fear — learnt from his relationship with his brother — that he will be physically punished for asserting himself.

III

The following shows Mike beginning to explore his relationship with one of the trainers. Until this exchange Mike had avoided making contact and had been content to stay with his projections.

Mike: (To Trainer 1) I feel suspicious of you . . . I don't trust you.

Trainer 1: Look at me and see if you can get in touch with your suspicion.

Mike: (Long silence — tilts his head to one side, then to the other, looking at the trainer from different angles). . . I can't put my finger on it.

Trainer 2: I have a suggestion . . . go up and put your finger on him.

Mike: (Gets up from his chair and places one finger on the trainer's shoulder, but avoids looking at him).

Trainer 2: As you do that look into his face.

Mike: (Follows the suggestion) . . . I feel my suspicion fading.

Trainer 2: How did you lose your suspicion?

Mike: By looking into his eyes.

By making contact at this simple level of touch, Mike found that the external world — in this case the trainer — was actually different from his internal picture. Having learnt this, Mike felt encouraged to discover more effective ways of making contact with others in the group.

CHAPTER 7

DEVELOPMENTS IN GESTALT

In order to understand some of the recent developments in Gestalt it is necessary to outline first its evolution in recent years. When Perls went to Esalen in the 1960's and began to run workshops and seminars for practising therapists his way of working — often described as the West Coast model — set a pattern that has been highly influential for other Gestalt therapists. This model still informs much of the Gestalt experience, both in a therapeutic and training setting, that is available in the UK. The nature of this model owes as much to Perls and the prevailing ethos of the 1960's — 'tune in, turn on, drop out' — as it does to Gestalt theory.

The characteristics of the *West Coast Model* are:

1. Group-based rather than one-to-one therapy (see pp. 21-2).
2. Emphasis on the experiential techniques (e.g. two chair work, dreams, etc.) rather than the methodology.
3. Emphasis on emotional expression and catharsis as an end in itself.
4. Charismatic leader who decides who to work with, and when and how to work. About 90% of the communication in the group is between the therapist and individual clients.
5. Little concern for group process. The therapist is not concerned with relationships in the group except as a starting position for individual work but he does pay a lot of attention to the client's relationship with the therapist. This pattern of working does often reinforce the role of the charismatic leader.
6. Strong emphasis on living for the now, i.e. encouraging the immediate gratification of individual needs.
7. Anti-intellectual by denigrating all thinking activities at the expense of emotional and sensory experience.
8. Emphasis on instant enlightenment and behaviour change.

Implied in this model is the assumption that all that is required to achieve change is a willingness to take risks and express feelings.

The undoubted genius of Perls plus the appropriateness of this model in the 1960's led to the creation of many 'little Fritzs' who popularized the techniques of Gestalt but lacked an understanding of the methodology. One consequence of this was the attempt in the 1970's to 'integrate' and 'support' the perceived inadequacies of Gestalt with other humanistic approaches. During this period therapists began offering Gestalt *plus* workshops (i.e. *plus* Bodywork; Transactional Analysis, Encounter, Spirituality, etc.)

In the late 1970's and early 1980's there was a move back to the original theory and a re-discovery of a more balanced approach.

Some of the more important changes have been:

1. Re-instatement of the theoretical base of Gestalt. Many current practitioners[1] have begun to clarify and develop the theory with a view to developing a clearer methodology. An important contribution in this area, the Dialogic Relationship, is described later in this chapter. In similar vein, there is now a recognition that in working with individuals the whole range of thinking activities have equal value to the range of emotional and sensory experiences. This brings Gestalt more clearly into the wider stream of learning theory which recognizes that effective learning requires reflection and conceptualization as well as experimentation and experience.

2. A different attitude to clients and trainees through greater emphasis on empathy and inclusion. The old Gestalt attitude of frustrating the client's patterns of behaviours does remain but it is now tempered with both kindness and clarity from the therapist.

3. There is also a return to the main objective of developing awareness of what is happening moment by moment in preference to awareness as the prerequisite to experimentation and risk taking.

4. Strong move away from the charismatic leader who both controls and delights the group with wizardry. Groups are more interactive and the therapist is more ready and willing to work with the group process (e.g. pairing-up, flight/fight, dependency, etc.) in addition to individual work.

5. Clear recognition that effective personal change requires time, that the insights and experiences that take place in groups are a means to an end and not an end in themselves. Learning to own undiscovered parts of the self and experimenting with new patterns of behaviour in the supportive atmosphere of a group need to be integrated by the individual and adapted for use in the world outside. For example, the person who learns to express anger for the first time by focusing on a cushion could simply 'transfer' that experience and end up treating people as cushions.

These changes in the area of therapy reflect our experiences at the College in the process of clearly adapting a group therapy model for use in interpersonal skills training. For example, on all programmes where the Gestalt approach is used when we do not offer formal theory inputs we attempt to offer a conceptual explanation to individuals about the work we have undertaken together. We also recognize and work at the level of what is happening to the group as well as with the individuals. Finally, in all our programmes the last half day is spent on a structured back-home planning activity which is designed to facilitate the transfer of learning.

The Dialogic Relationship[2]

As mentioned earlier in this chapter there has been a considered move away from techniques in favour of working with a methodological approach based on Gestalt principles. Central to this approach is the Gestalt concept of contact which has been defined as 'touching with mutual awareness of differences'. As an activity contact involves — connecting, merging, separating and withdrawing. There are four basic aspects of effective contact:

1. It involves the senses (hearing, touch, taste, smell, seeing).
2. There is a need for separation (if I stay too long I become confluent with the other person).
3. There is a need for movement (i.e. toward and away from, as a natural cycle like sleeping and waking).
4. The awareness of differences between self and other.

The objective in Gestalt is to establish this pattern of contact, i.e. a Dialogic Relationship, between trainer and course member. There are five characteristics of this type of relationship.

1. *Inclusion*

The trainer makes contact with the trainee and at the same time allows himself to be affected by the trainee and the trainee's experiences as they occur moment by moment. He attempts to see the world through the trainee's eyes. To do this effectively the trainer needs to 'bracket', i.e. lay on one side, his own experiences, perceptions, values and beliefs. In broad terms this is similar to Carl Rogers' idea of unconditional acceptance.

2. *Presence*

The trainer respects his true self sufficiently to know it, maintain it, while practising inclusion, and to show it rather than 'seeming', i.e. dissonance between what is experienced and what is shown. For example, the trainer who is very concerned and wants to look neutral or who is scared and wants to look calm is 'seeming' rather than present. By working in the present, the trainer is willing to offer his moment by moment experiences — feelings, thoughts, distractions, physical sensations — as information to the course member. Some of his responses will be about those parts of the course member that are outside his awareness. For example, offering feedback about suppressed anger or attempts by the course member to manipulate the trainér.

3. *Commitment to Dialogue*

A commitment to dialogue not only means each expresses his inner self to the other and is also receptive to the other's self-expression, but it specifically means allowing the outcome to be determined by what happens rather than allow it to be controlled by either individual. This means a relationship of mutual influence and as such is likely to challenge the trainer's need to be in control or the course member's need to be dependent.

4. *Non-Exploitation*

The Gestalt approach is a non-exploitative and non-manipulative person to person relationship in which the trainer regards each person as an end in himself. Although mutality in training is not complete and there is a differentiation of task/role, there is no hierarchical status system encouraged or entered into by the trainer. There are four forms of exploitation:

1. The person treated as a means to an end. For example, to be categorized; to be used to encourage the others; to meet the ego needs of the trainer.
2. An inequality of language. The course member needs to understand *how* he is learning as well as *what* he is learning.
3. The trainer not doing his job properly by not taking responsibility for his self or working beyond his limits.
4. Failure to respond to appropriate limits as determined by the sensitivities of the course member, e.g. teasing about one aspect of behaviour, of which the trainee is ashamed.

5. *Living the Relationship*

Contacting is living rather than talking about living. It is doing and experiencing rather than analysing. It is sharing an experience here and now which has been mutually shaped by both parties and leads to learning for each.

References

1. For examples see *The Gestalt Journal*, p. 46.
2. *Adapted* from 'Gestalt therapy: a dialogic method' by Gary M. Yontef, Faculty Member of the Los Angeles Institute of Gestalt Therapy.

CHAPTER 8

EXPLORATIONS

The following exercises are invitations for the reader to explore who he is and how he relates to the world. Like any other exploration the reader is likely to experience both the discomforts and pleasures of discovery. Some of the possible discomforts are:

 (i) an intensity of feeling — anger, sadness, despair, loss etc.
 (ii) sudden awareness of 'forgotten' experiences.
(iii) sense of isolation.

It is important that the reader pays attention to his need for support before beginning these exercises. The normal support available in a group from other members and an experienced trainer needs to be at hand. The development of an individual in Gestalt terms, involves moving from a position of depending on the environment for support to the ability to take the initiative in gaining the support needed from the environment. The types of support available are:

(1) Self-support Systems:
  — pay attention to your breathing, at moments of discomfort support
    yourself with a few deep breaths. The exercise on breathing describes an
    effective technique. Pay particular attention to the problem of hyper-
    ventilation, i.e. taking in too much oxygen rapidly and failing to exhale.
    Always breathe evenly.
  — pay attention to your physical support. When sitting ensure that your
    body is evenly supported across all points of contact with the floor or
    the chair.
  — be willing to accept who you are. Many people put themselves under
    considerable pressure to be different in some way and consequently
    give themselves a bad time.
  — give yourself permission to be who you are. One effective way of accept-
    ing who you are is to give yourself permission to be. So say out loud, 'I
    give myself permission to be me' until you are satisfied.

(2) External Support
  The most important form of external support for these exercises is to do
  them with someone you trust and who is prepared to offer you
  — time
  — permission to be who you are

- acceptance
- care and comfort

It is recommended that the reader takes responsibility for availing himself of both types of support.

Awareness Exercises (Five minutes for each exercise)

(1) Take some time to pay attention to your awareness now. Let your awareness wander and say out loud, 'Now I am aware of...', and finish the sentence. As you shift your awareness to different events continue speaking and prefix each statement with, 'Now I am aware of...'.

(2) After a few minutes review your statements. Is your awareness largely concerned with external events (sounds in the room, the furniture, floor, windows etc), with fantasy activity (remembering, thinking of the future, imagining etc), or with your feelings? If it is directed in one area take some time to attend to the other areas. Continue to prefix each statement with 'Now I am aware of...'. As you do this pay attention to how you interrupt yourself, e.g. deciding that the exercise is too hard, or pointless, or thinking about what else you could be doing. Again, after a few minutes, review your experiences.

(3) Now take a few minutes and start to direct your awareness. Imagine that your awareness is like a spotlight bringing into view some experiences and leaving others to merge into darkness. Start each sentence: 'Now I choose to be aware of...'. How easy or difficult did you find the process of directing your awareness? How did you interrupt the process?

(4) With this exercise let your awareness wander again but pay attention to your feelings. Start each sentence with 'Now I am aware of... and I feel... (happy, sad, pleasant, uncomfortable)'.

Every experience that we have (looking at a table, touching fabric, smelling coffee, listening to a typewriter, eating an orange) has some emotional quality for us. The purpose of this exercise is to bring into awareness the emotional qualities of everyday experiences we take for granted.

Breathing Exercise (20-30 minutes)

For the most effective way of experiencing this exercise, it is suggested that you prepare as follows:

(1) Loosen any tight or restrictive clothing (pay particular attention to shirt collars and waist fastenings) and take off your shoes.

(2) Lie down on your back on the floor. (Too soft a surface, such as a bed, will, paradoxically, leave you feeling unsupported).

(3) Keep your head raised about 3″ above the floor. A book beneath your head should be sufficient.

(4) Raise your knees from the floor, keeping the soles of your feet flat on the ground. Now gently collapse one knee against the other so both are gently supported.

(5) Place the palm of your left hand on your abdomen.

(6) Important note – pay particular attention to the problem of hyperventilation, i.e. taking in too much oxygen at a fast rate. Always breathe evenly. At the first sign of dizziness or numbness in the extremities, i.e. fingers and toes – discontinue exercise.

Now close your eyes and find a comfortable position . . . Take some time to become aware of your body . . . Do you feel evenly supported at all the places where your body is in contact with the floor (soles of your feet, buttocks, elbows, shoulders?) . . . Take your time to find a more balanced position . . .

Now inhale slowly . . . feel the stream of air as it passes through your mouth, into your throat, and then into your lungs . . . As your lungs fill up with air your left hand will begin to rise as your abdomen expands . . .

When you have completed the breath, slowly begin to exhale . . . Feel the stream of air as it begins the return journey from your lungs, into your throat, and out through your mouth . . . As the air is expelled make it into a sound. Make sure that you breathe all the way out and breathe in only when you feel the need for more air.

Continue to inhale and exhale in this way . . . take only the breath you need. As you continue with the exercise pay attention to any blockages or resistances to your breathing . . . When they occur do not try to break through them with your breathing but begin to explore them with your awareness . . . Take time to get to know the block . . . What does the block feel like? . . . When you are familiar with the block accept it as part of you . . . When you have accepted it let it go and continue to explore the experience of breathing . . .

When you have explored enough turn gently onto your side and rest. When you feel sufficiently rested, very slowly begin the process of returning to a sitting position . . . Be gentle with yourself.

Topdog--Underdog Dialogue (20 minutes at least)

Sit comfortably and close your eyes . . . Now imagine that you are looking at yourself, sitting in front of you . . . Form some kind of picture of yourself, sitting in front of you . . . How are you sitting? . . . What are you wearing? . . . What facial expression do you see? Now begin to criticize this image of yourself as if you are talking to another person... Speak out loud and begin each sentence with the words, 'You should...', or, 'You should not..'... Make a long list of criticism... Listen to your voice as you do this... Allow yourself to feel, emotionally and physically, as you do this...

Now change places with this image and begin to answer the criticisms... Speak out loud your response to these criticisms... Again, listen to your voice as you do this... Express yourself emotionally and physically as you do this... Switch roles whenever you want to, but keep the dialogue going... Notice all the details of what is going on as you do this... Notice how the two roles begin to develop... Notice if they speak to one another or at each other... See what changes, if any, occur in the dialogue...

At the end of the dialogue review your experiences. How familiar are you with these two conflicting parts? Does this dialogue remind you of internal conversations that you have experienced before? Does one of the roles remind you of someone from your past – a parent, relation, teacher? If you do recognize someone in the dialogue begin the exercise again, but speak directly to the imagined person concerned.

If the conflict is unresolved between the two parts then resume the dialogue. What is topdog prepared to offer in the resolution? What is underdog willing to do? It is important in the integration of such conflicts that both parties feel satisfied by any agreements. If either party is left with the smallest possible amount of dissatisfaction, then the conflict is unresolved.

Introjects (50 minutes)

Spend 10 minutes or so reviewing your experiences at work. Consider a typical day and how you behave at work. When you have done so then write down ten statements beginning: 'At work I have to...' (e.g. be punctual).

When you have completed the list go back to each statement and add to each a further statement beginning: 'or else...' (e.g. 'At work I have to be punctual or else... (my boss will reprimand me).

Then go back to your amended list and turn each statement into a sentence beginning: 'I choose to... because..'. (e.g. 'I choose to be punctual because... it is the most effective way of managing my time').

Finally, go back to your original 'have to' statements. Who gave you this rule? Does this rule still make any sense to you? The rules that you had difficulties with in turning into 'choose to' statements need careful review. Does your 'choose to' statement conceal another rule? e.g. 'I choose to be punctual because ... punctuality impresses my subordinates'.

Review each of your final statements until you feel satisfied with the answer.

Projections (20 minutes)

(1) Think of someone at work you like and/or admire very much. Then write down the qualities that you like and/or admire, e.g. He is honest.
(2) Think of someone at work you dislike intensely. Then write down the qualities that you dislike, e.g. He is lazy.
(3) Having completed the two lists say out loud those qualities about yourself, e.g. I am honest, I am lazy.

As you make these statements about yourself pay attention to your feelings, emotionally and physically, and listen to the tone and quality of your voice. What clues do you have that these statements contain qualities that you disown in yourself by projecting them onto others?

Confluence (30 minutes)

Review a typical day at work. What time do you arrive? What time do you leave? Are there certain rituals that you go through? (walking the same way to work; starting each day with a cup of coffee?) To whom do you regularly talk? Do you always say the same types of statements? Is your office or desk always laid out in the same way (very ordered, disordered)? Do you set about tasks in the same order each day? Do you always go to lunch at the same time every day?

When you have identified all these patterns of behaviour and habits that you follow take time to consider which, if any, are the most efficient or satisfying ways of spending your time. Experiment by trying to change one of the behaviours. How do you feel as you try something different? Do you feel pleasure, resistance, anxiety, excitement at the prospect of change?

We take for granted that these patterns were spontaneously acquired, but attempts to change them bring us up against resistances so strong as to be unmistakable evidence of unhealthy confluence.

Retroflections (20 minutes)

Think of the last times that you experienced some, or all, of the following:
(1) punishing yourself
(2) congratulating yourself
(3) angry with yourself
(4) felt self pity
(5) felt inadequate
(6) distrusted yourself

For each of the occasions you have identified, remember who else was involved. For each incident identify the real target of your retroflected feeling.

(1) Who did you want to punish?
(2) From whom did you want congratulation?
(3) With whom were you really angry?
(4) For whom did you feel pity? or
    From whom did you want pity?
(5) Who should have felt inadequate?
(6) Who did you really distrust?

Deflections (25 minutes)

Think of a recent occasion at work when you came away from a meeting or interview feeling dissatisfied. Reflect on what you said at that meeting. Identify any examples of:

(1) minimization – e.g. 'It's not really important'
(2) grandiosity – e.g. 'If we don't act now the project will be destroyed'
(3) generalization – e.g. 'Anyone would be angry in this situation'
(4) intellectualization – e.g. 'It is likely that I am being defensive'
(5) diplomacy – e.g. 'Let's move on'

After listing examples write against each what you really meant or said

e.g. 'It's not really important' – 'This is important to me'

Then read out loud each of your revised statements.

CHAPTER 9

GLOSSARY OF TERMS

Contact/Boundary   Contacting is the process of sensing, feeling, assimilating, rejecting, touching, communicating, conflicting etc. Contact takes place at the boundary, i.e. the line of distinction between the organism (man) and the environment.

Continuum of
Awareness   Training technique which involves the individual expressing his experiences as he becomes aware of them.

Deflection   Moving away from saying what you mean, expressing what you feel, making contact with another person.

Emotion   Feelings – guide to interests, needs, concerns.

Experiment   Term applied to the process of an individual trying out, for him, new behaviour. The validation of an experiment is determined by the individual's sense of satisfaction.

Fantasy   Term applied to any activity which does not deal with here-and-now experience. Therefore embraces all thinking activity (remembering, anticipating, guessing, intellectualizing, interpreting etc). Term is often used in training groups to prefix an interpretation or guess, e.g. 'My fantasy is that you are angry now'.

Figure/Ground   Figure is the focus of interest which is distinguished from the setting or context, i.e. ground. Describes the process by which gestalten emerge and, if completed, dissolve into the ground.

Gestalt   Generally, a pattern or configuration. Particularly a need, interest or concern seeking satisfaction. *Plural* – gestalten.

Hot Seat   Training technique by which an empty chair is placed in the group. When someone in the group wishes to work they go and sit in the chair. By extension, any individual doing a piece of work can be described as sitting in the 'hot seat'.

Introjection   Uncritical acceptance of rules or patterns of behaviour which are imposed by parents, teachers, organizations etc.

Projection   Imagining that our own (unwanted) feelings belong to someone else.

Retroflection   Turning inwards on ourselves, feelings that are really directed at someone else, e.g. instead of expressing anger we punish ourselves with feelings of inadequacy.

Topdog-Underdog	The topdog is the authoritarian part of ourselves which sets down the rules. The underdog is the whiney and manipulative part of ourselves which undermines the topdog.
Two-chair Work	Training technique which involves the individual acting out a dialogue between two, or more, conflicting parts of himself. Often the dialogue is a Topdog-Underdog conflict.
Unfinished Business	The debris of incomplete gestalten which litter our relationships with other people. Consists of unexpressed feelings or concerns and unsatisfied needs.

BIBLIOGRAPHY

1. DOWNING, Jack. *Editor. Gestalt awareness: papers from the San Francisco Gestalt Institute.* Perennial Library, New York, 1976. pp. 161.

    Papers covering range of subjects — Gestalt for trainers, women and Gestalt, use of language, dreams etc. Has no index.

2. FAGAN, Joen and SHEPHERD, Irma Lee. *Editors. Gestalt Therapy now: Theory, Techniques, Applications.* Penguin, 1972. pp. 380.

    Papers by therapists, including Perls. Also contains biographical notes on contributors; annotated bibliography; and descriptions of training tapes and films. Index.

3. FEDER, Bud and RONALL, Ruth. *Editors. Beyond the Hot Seat: Gestalt Approaches to Group.* Brunner/Magell, New York, 1980. pp. 256.

    Papers concerned with the integration of Gestalt with group dynamics in a wide range of clinical, educational and community settings. Bibliography, notes on contributors and index.

4. HATCHER, Chris and HIMELSTEIN, Philip. *Editors. The Handbook of Gestalt Therapy.* Jason Arunson, New York, 1976. pp. 809.

    Contains reprints of selections from most of the important literature. There are four major sections: the contribution of Perls; contemporary theory; techniques and perspectives; and resources. The third section looks at the integration of Gestalt with other approaches (T.A., Biofeedback, Bioenergetics, Organization Development). The resource section (literature, tapes, films) is particularly good. Has separate name and subject indexes.

5. HERMAN, Stanley M. and KORENICH, Michael. *Authentic Management: a Gestalt Orientation to Organisations and their Development.* Addison-Wesley 1977. pp. 236.

    Describes some of the Gestalt concepts and relates them to issues in organizational life. Also contains exercises, case studies and identifies key issues in the consultancy process. No index.

6. MARCUS, Eric H. *Gestalt Therapy and Beyond: an Integrated Mind-Body Approach.* Meta Publications, California, 1979. pp. 253.

    Concerned with how Gestalt can be integrated with other approaches — Neo-Reichian body work, guided imagery and psychodrama. No index.

7. PASSONS, William R. *Gestalt Approaches in Counselling.* Holt, Rinehart and Winston, New York, 1975. pp. 239.

    Includes model of counselling, some Gestalt theory, but concentrates on awareness, language, non-verbal behaviour, fantasy, thinking, feelings, as dimensions of the counselling relationship. Includes exercises. Index.

8. PERLS, Frederick S. *Ego, Hunger and Aggression: the Beginning of Gestalt Therapy.* Vintage Books, New York, 1969. pp. 273.

   Seminal work which describes Perls' transition from Freudian psychoanalysis to the Gestalt approach.

9. PERLS, Frederick S. *The Gestalt Approach and Eyewitness to Therapy.* Bantam, 1976. pp. 209.

   Two books in one volume. 'The Gestalt Approach' is a readable introduction to Gestalt theory: 'Eyewitness to Therapy' contains transcripts of training films made by Perls. No index.

10. PERLS, Frederick S., HEFFERLINE, Ralph F. and GOODMAN, Paul. *Gestalt Therapy: Excitement and Growth in the Human Personality.* Pelican, 1973. pp. 535.

    The standard work on Gestalt therapy. Contains a series of experiments for developing self-awareness, and a critique of psychoanalysis. Difficult to read more than a few pages at a time. No index.

11. PERLS, Frederick S. *Gestalt Therapy Verbatim.* Real People Press, Utah, 1969. pp. 279.

    Transcripts of seminars and workshops run by Perls at the Esalen Institute from 1966 to 1968. Also has long introduction on theory. No index.

12. PERLS, Frederic S. *In and Out the Garbage Pail.* Bantam Books, 1972. pp. 298.

    Autobiography written as a flow of awareness. Idiosyncratic style but very readable.

13. POLSTER, Erving and POLSTER, Miriam. *Gestalt Therapy Integrated: Contours of Theory and Practice.* Vintage Books, New York, 1974. pp. 329.

    Good introduction to the theory with a briefer outline of some training techniques. Also contains a few introductory exercises for training groups. No index.

14. SCHIFFMAN, Muriel. *Gestalt Self-Therapy: and Further Techniques for Personal Growth.* Self-Therapy Press, California, 1971. pp. 223.

    Programme approach to Gestalt therapy. Contains exercises and transcripts. No index.

15. SIMKIN, James S. *Gestalt Therapy Mini-Lectures.* Celestial Arts, California, 1976. --. 124.

    Very good and readable book — particularly for the trainer. Concerned with Gestalt in groups, theoretical and practical issues, training techniques, dream work, and clinical work. Bibliography. No index.

16. SMITH, Edward W. L. *Editor. The Growing Edge of Gestalt Therapy.* Citadel Press, New Jersey, 1977. pp. 239.

    Covers the origins of Gestalt therapy, innovations in therapy, Gestalt and other approaches (Jungian psychology, hypnosis, synergy and Eastern philosophy). Has notes on contributors and an index.

17. STEVENS, Barry. *Don't Push the River*. Real People Press, Utah, 1970. pp. 269.

An account of the author's use of Gestalt with the ways of Zen, Krishnamurti and the American Indian.

18. STEVENS, John O. *Awareness: Exploring, Experimenting, Experiencing*. Bantam, 1973. pp. 310.

Contains over 100 experiments for developing awareness. Exercises for individuals, pairs and groups. Very useful training resource.

19. STEVENS, John O. *Editor. Gestalt is: a Collection of Articles*. Bantam, 1977. pp. 286.

Contains a collection of specialist articles chosen simply on the basis of the editor's interest. Includes some of Perls' previously unpublished papers. No index.

20. ZINKER, Joseph. *Creative Process in Gestalt Therapy*. Vintage Books, New York, 1978. pp. 283.

Describes the author's use of creative approaches in the therapeutic process (e.g. use of imagery, metaphor, guided fantasy and art). Also contains a bibliography and an index.

Journals

THE GESTALT JOURNAL

Published twice a year by the Center for Gestalt Development, Inc.

The Gestalt Journal
P.O. Box 990
Highland
New York 12528
USA

Vol. 1. 1978.

Serious and academic articles on the theory and practise of Gestalt Therapy.